DESIGN WITH THE LAND

LANDSCAPE ARCHITECTURE OF MICHAEL VAN VALKENBURGH

Harvard University Graduate School of Design

Princeton Architectural Press

ISBN 1-56898-022-1
Library of Congress Card Catalog Number:
94-76576

*Design with the Land: Landscape Architecture of
Michael Van Valkenburgh* is the first in a series of
Harvard University Graduate School of Design
publications on contemporary landscape architecture. We acknowledge the generous support
of Helen and Kimball Whitney, the Lawrence
Halprin Fund, and the Daniel Urban Kiley Fund.

Published in the United States of America by
Princeton Architectural Press, Inc.
37 East 7th Street
New York, New York 10003
212 995.9620

Printed in Canada

C O N T E N T S

WITH TIME IN MIND

THE MODERN LANDSCAPES OF MICHAEL VAN VALKENBURGH

Peter G. Rowe

Shortly after the beginning of this century, the spatial aspect within the conjunction of space and time that characterized much modern architecture and landscape architecture often bore a distinct temporal trace. The canons of early modernism, for instance, steadfastly eschewed commitments to past practices, promulgated a progressive technological view of progress, and insisted on primacy of the zeitgeist in most matters of expression. Perceptually, space was often represented through simultaneous presentation from otherwise disparate viewpoints, as in cubist landscapes, or through formal geometrical abstraction of contemporary material conditions, as in many functionalist designs from the machine age. By contrast, toward the end of this century, especially with the alleged postmodern break from an earlier modernism, a more expansive idea of time in the space/time manifold of contemporary environments has become routinely the subject of spatial representation. Conceptual links back in time are made, for instance, through various figural references. A concern for present context is reflected often, through design, by magnifying spatial differences between one locale and another, rather than by rendering them through the universalizing lens of earlier modernism. In short, time is now bearing a more generous spatial trace.

The landscape architecture of Michael Van Valkenburgh is unabashedly modern in many of its spatial concepts, uses of materials, and geometrical abstractions. Of more interest is the sustained spatial speculation about time and temporal phenomena to be found in the work. Firmly anchored intellectually in the modernist tradition, Michael Van Valkenburgh has been advancing and expanding the concept of landscape architecture by steadfastly addressing the matter of time and its spatial expression.

There are several temporal preoccupations that are striking in Van Valkenburgh's projects. First and perhaps most obvious is the spatial and visual registration of natural processes and associated temporal changes. Both the Radcliffe Ice Walls and the Krakow Ice Garden poetically yet directly record seasonal fluctuations. A similar seasonal registration can be found in the entry landscape for the General Mills Headquarters, where grasses are deliberately burnt off and then renewed in an annual cycle. Moreover, one frequently finds less mechanical and more symbolic references to seasonal, diurnal, and circadian rhythms in the vegetative borders of the Pucker Garden, the hedgerows of the early Eudoxia project, and in the respect for Le Nôtre's 'Rooms of Light' at the Jardin des Tuileries.

Registration of continuity with past practices, respect for tradition, and a willing use of precedents can also be found in several projects. Mill Race Park deliberately recalls the industrial history of Columbus, Indiana, through revelation of old site fragments from that era, and the Jardin des Tuileries is understandably respectful of Le Nôtre's original proposal. More abstractedly and less by approbation, static spatial geometries of existing landscapes are modified through the use of temporal-spatial devices like the dissolution of the formal room-like geometry at the Minneapolis Sculpture Garden Extension into a fragmented sequence of experiences, spatially depicting, as it were, the impact of some event visited on the former formal order. Indirectly, selection of an ecologically appropriate palette of plant materials at the General Mills Headquarters and a regional garden at Lake Minnetonka, spatially arrest any universal temporal quality in either of these projects.

Finally, explicit spatial registration of the growth, change, and flux that accompanies almost any landscape is thoroughly explored. At Mill Race Park, for instance, the underlying flood-plain ecology is made spatially visible by the presence of a circular pond, the edge of which clearly demarks temporal fluctuations in weather patterns and surface water levels. The permanence and, indeed, nobility of granite walls, border edges, and the like, at General Mills, in the Sackler Garden, and in the Avenue Montaigne Courtyard also act as a datum against which periodic shifts and cycles of plant and other ground materials can be gauged. Conversely, the projective qualities of the HO-AM Sculpture Garden spatially define future sites of works yet to be acquired.

MICHAEL VAN VALKENBURGH

A CLIENT'S PERSPECTIVE

Will Miller

I first met Michael Van Valkenburgh when he came to Columbus, Indiana—the small midwestern town where I live—to interview with the Parks and Recreation Department for the commission to design Mill Race Park. The Parks Department had applied to the Cummins Engine Foundation for a grant from its architectural program. Under this program, the foundation pays the design fees for local public projects if the architect or landscape architect is chosen from a list supplied by the foundation of the best designers in the country.

Although I was not a member of the client committee making the selection of architects, I was allowed to sit in on the presentations. What struck me as I looked at Van Valkenburgh's slides and listened to him speak was that here was a person capable of designing memorable landscapes. With the exception of the works of Dan Kiley and Roberto Burle Marx, or of Russell Page's sculpture grounds for PepsiCo, there have been very few modern landscapes that have moved me and entered into my memory the way certain works of Capability Brown, Olmsted, Le Nôtre, or the Zen masters have. Evidently, the client committee agreed, for Van Valkenburgh was the unanimous choice to receive the commission.

What was so appealing to me and the client group? It is hard to be precise. Like Kiley, everything about a landscape by Van Valkenburgh seems intentional. His use of rows, grids, and quincunxes boldly asserts that this is a "manmade" landscape. Yet he does not depend on exotic specimens for this effect. He identifies species commonly found in the area and then makes them an inexorable part of his design.

At the same time, an essential part of the beauty of his designs is that, as often as one experiences them, there is always another layer of meaning to be discovered. Viewed one way, a row of trees in the garden he designed for my home appears Euclidean in its alignment and regularity. However, if you look from a different perspective, the apparent order fragments and becomes more naturalistic. Layering is literally used in his design for the Courthouse Square in Columbus (not yet constructed) where a grid of under-story trees is inserted among the irregularly spaced trunks of the existing canopy of mature trees in order to unite the entire composition.

Van Valkenburgh's designs are also rooted in a sense of place and the history of that place. Mill Race Park occupies an ox-bow in a river that is part of the flood plain. Ironically, before its redesign, one had almost no sense of the river that surrounds the park on three sides. Through the skillful relocation of pedestrian paths and the introduction of a large circular lake in the center of the park, Van Valkenburgh made water, and even flooding, a major presence in the park. He also reuses the remains of a foundation from a tannery as a low screening wall for a parking lot and creates large earthworks, which recall Native American burial mounds in the region, to serve as seating for spectators at the amphitheater and a basketball court.

In attempting to get a sense of the landscape architect and his landscapes from an exhibition—or from its catalogue—one is forced to recognize how inadequate both are to the task. Drawings, models, and photographs convey very little of the forces outside the control of the architect that shape the design process: client expectations, local politics, environmental regulations, budgets, and so forth. The elements of an exhibition are, at best, scraps from a writer's journal, unable to describe completely either the creative process or the completed novel itself. In landscape architecture, even more so than in architecture, it is impossible to separate the design from the process that created it.

Public landscapes, like Mill Race Park or the Front Door Project in Columbus, increasingly result not only from considerations of form, function, and economics, but also from politics. To build a public project, a landscape architect must be able to open up the creative process to participation by many constituencies, each of which has a stake in the outcome. He or she must listen

4

to these groups and respond in ways that convincingly take into account their concerns or solve their problems. The public client group has a significant responsibility to ensure that this is a positive process that improves the design, rather than watering it down to the least common denominator. For, after all, the designer has been hired for his or her ability to solve design problems and create images that the client and constituency groups cannot. In the end, the task before the designer is to express for the community or client in form and function what they could not express themselves. In the years we have been working together, I believe that both Van Valkenburgh (and his associates) and the client groups in Columbus have learned a great deal about making good design work in the public arena from interacting with each other.

It is difficult to conceive how large an impact seemingly small decisions made in the course of the design process can have. I once told Van Valkenburgh the story of some trees in my parents' garden. Nearly identical specimens of honey locusts were planted within a hundred feet of one another—two in an informal grouping in undisturbed soil, the rest in an allée on a terrace created by rearranging the natural topography. After 25 years, the informal trees had grown nearly twice as tall as the trees in the allée. When the latter were dug up, it was discovered that the clay soil in which the allée trees were planted had been compacted so much by the earth-moving equipment that created the terrace, the trees' roots had never been able to grow outside their original root balls. This story, Van Valkenburgh responded, gave him a more dynamic view of how landscapes are truly created than he had before. As we all know, landscape designs are not made once or twice, but are constantly being remade through the long-term consequences of construction techniques, the growth and death of plants, seasonal changes, people's use of the landscape, maintenance choices, and other factors not always contemplated at their creation.

Given all the aspects of the process of modern landscape design outside the control of the landscape architect, it is all the more remarkable when a moving and memorable landscape is created. To decide for yourself whether the designs shown here qualify, you will ultimately have to go and visit them. I can only assure you that, if your sensibilities are anything like mine, they will be worth the visit.

DESIGN WITH THE LAND

TIME, MATERIAL, AND EVENT

THE WORK OF MICHAEL VAN VALKENBURGH

James Corner

> Strange how things in the offing, once they're sensed,
> Convert to things foreknown;
> And how what's come upon is manifest
>
> Only in light of what has been gone through.
> Seventh heaven may be
> The whole truth of a sixth sense come to pass.
>
> At any rate, when light breaks over me
> The way it did on the road beyond Coleraine
> Where wind got saltier, the sky more hurried
>
> And silver lamé shivered on the Bann
> Out in mid-channel between the painted poles,
> That day I'll be in step with what escaped me.

The above extract, from the poem *Squarings* by Seamus Heaney, describes with great eloquence the kind of elusive and subtle experience that one often has when engaging a landscape. Here, the landscape is less an object or focus of attention and more a multi-dimensional geography that is slowly absorbed through habit and engagement over time. This knowing of a place through inhabitation differs significantly from the voyeuristic gaze of the tourist or the spectator, and it is this depth of experience that allows for the uncanny coalescence of newness with familiarity of which Heaney writes—in essence, a being (or, more precisely, a becoming) "at home." Here there is no shock of the new, no great epiphany, only an ever-emerging fullness in the lives of a landscape's occupants.

With a rare and graceful clarity, the built landscapes of Michael Van Valkenburgh modestly demonstrate these simple, though radical, premises: that the knowledge of a place derives more deeply through the experience of material, time, and event than through visuality alone, and that landscape experience is fuller and more profound when it accrues through inhabitation than through the immediacy of the image or the objectification of the new. Subsequently, questions about movement, tactility, seasonal change, and social encounter present greater challenges (and rewards) to the designer than do stylistic, scenographic, or avant-gardist concerns.

From his early preoccupations with ice walls and seasonally dynamic hedge gardens, Van Valkenburgh continues his quest to integrate the flow and flux of natural phenomena with social and programmatic life. His recent work, in particular, clearly strives to create stages for both natural and civic life, resisting the current tendency to think of landscape as a static scene or object of representation. As a consequence of the emphasis placed upon temporality, tactility, and occupancy, these sensuous and place-bound designs can never be adequately represented in photographs and drawings.

Particularly difficult for the camera to capture is the tactile nature of materials, especially as they play out with the passage of time. Demonstrated at the Pucker Garden and the courtyard garden at 50, avenue Montaigne, for example, is Van Valkenburgh's sensually eloquent use of materials. Plants, stones, gravels, metals, and water are arranged and presented in ways that provide an abundance of tactile conditions and social adjacencies. The sound, temperature, smell, touch, and weight of the materials provides the greater part of the experience of the place, while the visual is subsumed into the "whole" and not allowed to dominate. Moreover, materials are selected and manipulated in ways that appear both familiar (or traditional) and inventive. Senses of the past, especially in the Paris garden, resonate with a contemporary vitality and freshness.

This sense of time and memory in Van Valkenburgh's work often attains a special depth due to his remarkable knowledge of plants and organic life, their various seasonal changes, and modes of cultivation and growth. At the General Mills Corporate Headquarters, for example, the prairie grass "lawn" contained by a ring of birch trees demonstrates a dynamic, regional ecology. While the actual prairie is indeed abstracted here, it is, at the same time, made more real, as if rarefied. Burnt annually, the life of the field emerges anew every time, changing almost weekly as different grass and flower species come into bloom. Similarly, the feeling at 50, avenue Montaigne is one of a working garden, with plants constantly being tended, watered, pruned, tied, layered, grafted, and espaliered.

As in other projects by Van Valkenburgh, there is always this vibrant sense of life, growth, abundance, and change, often intensified through a contrast with more austere and unchanging elements, such as walls, steps, and platforms. Such contrast between change and permanence is exemplified in the circular lake at Mill Race Park, for example, which is an attempt to create a figure of resistance to the occasional flooding of the park from the adjacent river. The circle becomes both a symbol and a constant, an unchanging benchmark in a landscape of natural flux and uncertainty.

In more recent work, the poetics of material and time have been further heightened through special attention to civic engagement and events. The proposal for the Oakville Park Competition, for example, demonstrates a new level of social complexity in Van Valkenburgh's work, with dramatic and elegant earthforms being used to orchestrate particular types of socialization and civic adjacency. As a centerpiece, the powerfully tear-shaped lawn is tilted to catch the sun and look back toward the city. Its generous size and simplicity provide a rare sense of landscape expanse in the city while accommodating both large and small gatherings. Like other projects by Van Valkenburgh, the aspiration behind this park is that it unite the elemental life of nature with the psychological, social, and public life of city dwellers.

Clearly, material, time, and event are essential components for any appreciation of Michael Van Valkenburgh's work. There is a subtlety at play in his practice, a quiet and restrained calm that some critics have found too austere and minimal; but I believe that these terms derive from a strictly aesthetic set of expectations and fail to understand the elusive nature of dwelling and

occupancy over time. Van Valkenburgh's is a deeply traditional practice, less concerned with fashion and whim than with the recurrent difficulty of constructing a ground where culture can meet
meaningfully with the life and processes of nature. As this difficulty has persisted historically, we
might also say that Van Valkenburgh's is also an inventive practice, returning to traditional themes
to present them anew. Here, we might recall the poetic sensibility of which Heaney writes—
invention within tradition and revelation within the commonplace—but I think also that an obser-
vation made by Jean-Paul Sartre encapsulates the integrity of Van Valkenburgh's quest: "we must
invent the heart of things if we wish one day to discover it." That such a project rests within the
power of the material imagination, in the ability to find a deeper character, a greater reality, in
what is hidden than in what is visible, underlies the difficulty (and the genius) of Van
Valkenburgh's work.

PRIVATE VISIONS

THE GARDENS OF MICHAEL VAN VALKENBURGH

Paula Deitz

As a curator himself in the 1980s of exhibitions on American landscape architecture, Michael Van Valkenburgh has explored the private garden in the twentieth century—both real and visionary. "Like the house in architecture, the garden is a succinct design statement, offering a concise view of each designer's philosophy," he wrote at the time. In his world, the private garden is more than a setting or an appendage to a house. It is an independent laboratory of ideas, a synthesis of art and craftsmanship. If the experiment succeeds, the forms may be applied to the larger world of parks and public spaces, but the fresh inspiration belongs to the original compressed version.

"Ideas spring from our hearts and minds and are informed by history and culture and tempered with a keen knowledge of how the world is built," is how he describes the creative confrontation with a new space. Drawings reveal the immediacy of this experience and serve as the repository of ideas which may take years to execute. He views design on the land, even with natural materials, as an artifice tempered by the dimension of time.

Van Valkenburgh's expansive imagination incorporates his knowledge of historical precedents—what he calls "revisiting ideas from the past"—and an ability to respond to the uniqueness of a site and of how it relates to a regional environment. Private gardens allow him personal control, and their scale makes possible a complete exploration of design. Sometimes, he refines an experimental idea in the backyard of the gray clapboard house in Cambridge where his office is located next door to a former laundromat that serves as the drafting room for Michael Van Valkenburgh Associates.

Growing up in an agricultural community, Van Valkenburgh says, provided him with the comfort and ease to let landscapes look legible and manmade. He recalls first fantasizing about the

land as a boy when he brought the cows home from pasture in the Catskills to his family's modest dairy farm in Lexington, New York. Today, his work retains what he sees as "the deliberate simplicity of that remembered agrarian landscape," as in the way a plantation of trees is angled into the hillside. For him, beauty and elegance are found in the straightforward solution rather than in the contrived picturesque. His search for a realistic approach, he believes, complements the abstract ideas he develops in his academic life, where design is taught as an art form.

At the beginning of his career, he was inspired by the book *Design and Nature* by Ian L. McHarg, the University of Pennsylvania landscape architect in the vanguard of the ecology movement who describes manmade landscapes as a picture of nature devised by both conscience and art. McHarg also offers the theory that we continually seek out or recreate "reassuring landscapes," images made memorable through past associations. In his own work, Van Valkenburgh refers to memory and narrative. Seen in succession, his gardens are woven together by threads of repeated themes and images that recall in minimal forms archetypal models.

In these private landscapes, he combines horticulture—both as a strong element of design and as a transition to natural plantings at the fringes—with a seductive use of mineral elements—stone, water, and metal—that bring a cool, tangible veneer to the settings. Finally, he adds levels, dramatic changes of level that suggest passage and journeys through the gardens. As at the Potager du Roi, the King's kitchen garden at Versailles, steep staircases and slopes make abrupt shifts in the viewer's perspective and repeatedly alter the experience of space.

In the birch garden he designed in Chestnut Hill, Massachusetts, he drew on his agrarian sensibility to resolve the problem of a sloping terrain behind the house by creating a grade change that was even more pronounced. From a flat terrace above, defined by a brick-and-bluestone retaining wall, a plain flight of wooden stairs plunges into the lower-story woodland garden. The steps evoke for Van Valkenburgh the rickety ones leading down to docks on Martha's Vineyard, where he spends weekends and summers, and they function visually like a drawbridge lowered as a connector.

Planted along the steep slopes on either side is a thick grove of multi-stem gray and white birch trees whose trunks angle out into linear designs against lush underplantings of rhododendron, mountain laurel, ferns, vinca, common periwinkle, and European ginger. In this deliberate quotation from the garden Fletcher Steele designed in 1926 at Naumkeag in Stockbridge, Massachusetts, Van Valkenburgh pays tribute to Steele's ideas about massing with subtle irregularity and about grading land in sculptural rather than natural forms.

While at Naumkeag the birch trees are seen in counterpoint to a series of curving stair rails of white pipes, in the Chestnut Hill garden the birch grove is bisected by a traditional Japanese temple path of diamond-shaped stepping stones set into bluestone gravel scattered with pine needles. Similar to the long granite stones that line Japanese paths, like one at Nanzen-ji in Kyoto, Van Valkenburgh has edged his path with black brick manganese, two dark lines that lead serenely not to a temple pavilion but to a stele cum fountain of polished green granite. Visible through a slit on the face of the stone column are overlapping plates of stainless steel that step up so that the flow of water cascades down over them as a fluid surface. At night, neon lights attached vertically in pairs to the brick piers at the top of the stairs cast an eerie glow akin to moonlight. This garden goes beyond pleasure by offering ideas and images that heighten one's experience of traversing what is otherwise a simple grove of trees.

As if designed as a continuation to the birch garden, the Pucker Garden, in nearby Brookline, evolved as a hillside embankment that creates an ascent in the shallow space of a suburban backyard. Calling on references to Roman antiquity, the garage at one side now appears like a ruin of an old tomb that has been excavated out of the adjacent hillside. Echoing the wooden steps, a staircase in high-tech galvanized steel checkerplate floats up like a shiny ziggurat across the myrtle-covered hillside. Curved like an amphitheater and planted with single-stem shadblow trees, the embankment becomes an ideal foil for displaying abstract sculptures on pedestals. The arrangement calls to mind the 1962 exhibition of David Smith's Voltri sculptures arrayed on the steps of the ancient coliseum in Spoleto, Italy.

Like the modernist architects of this century, Van Valkenburgh subscribes to the aesthetic principle that new materials and the latest technology dictate new forms. Without relinquishing classical garden features, he introduces hard-edged structures and industrial surfaces that at first appear more practical than ornamental, except that in the end their trimness and suitability make them a perfect blend with the flat green expanses that are to his gardens what sleek glass is to architecture.

At the entrance to the Pucker Garden, and on axis with the floating staircase across the lawn, a progression of Japanese-style stepping stones has been abstracted into rectangular stones of varying lengths embedded into exposed aggregate concrete. Running crosswise between these pavers are inlaid bands of irregularly set black pebbles that mimic Japanese stepping-stone patterns. Further on, the rendered surfaces of gray stucco for the retaining wall of the formed hillside and the garage exterior complement the galvanized steel post-and-wire-mesh trellis for Boston ivy that screens the back of the viewing path around the top of the hill. Guests usually complete the garden circuit on the flat terrace roof of the garage with its balustrade also of galvanized steel and wire mesh. From this overlook, the Japanese stone entrance patio below resembles a Mondrian painting in tones of gray.

In the lee of a 1950s modern house on a waterside estate in Greenwich, Connecticut, Van Valkenburgh continued the play of hard and soft surfaces in another sculpture garden he created to display important works by Barbara Hepworth. Concealed from the outer drive by a brick serpentine wall that provides slots for the carpark, the bluestone path inside the enclosure swings around a central island of Vinca minor in what the landscape architect calls a gestural curve. Except for an existing cutleaf maple he retained to preside over one corner, the sculptures are the main vertical features in the landscape. With the sound of low spouting fountain jets along the center of a rectangular goldfish pond, the space recalls old cloistered gardens, fresh but simple with dark beds of ivy around the perimeter.

Some of these same qualities are present in his Black Granite Garden in Los Angeles, only here the inspiration might be Italian cypress allées or Moorish rills. Even where the images refer to historical precedents, the forms are classically minimal. This is a linear garden, a 120-foot avenue of twenty-foot-high columnar Italian cypress trees set in beds of needle point ivy along a central spine of rosy gray manganese brick pavers that appears infinitely long, channeled as it is between the tall trees. At the edge of a small rill parallel to the path, another granite stele fountain has a monolithic quality—the water pours down the created "washboard" side, while the rough side, dry, faces the sun. A wall of thick-trunked ficus trees forms the boundary along the entire length of the garden. Length like this in a defined landscape is a liberating quality. The reason why avenues in general are so inviting is that they appear to go on forever.

One of Van Valkenburgh's wittiest designs is for a client in St. Louis who collects art from the commercial memorabilia of American highway strips—the real Pop Art. Among his treasures is a red metal Pegasus, the mythological flying steed that is the logo for the Mobil Company. As the myth goes, Pegasus with a single stroke of his hoof could bring forth the waters of Hippocrene, the sacred fountain of the Muses on Mount Helicon that brought them poetic inspiration. This is a symbolic garden ornament for all times. Van Valkenburgh has treated it as the pinnacle of a garden experience that begins with a long granite walk on the street side that passes under a connecting passageway between two house structures and continues as a bridge across a sunken garden to the terminus, the flying Pegasus soaring appropriately across a fountain pool on a metal arch.

Four years ago, Michael Van Valkenburgh began working on Martha's Vineyard and fell in love with its magical landscape of agricultural fields and stands of oak trees stunted by the force of prevailing winds. After coming to the island and eventually buying a house there, he came to see the natural landscape as more powerful than anything he could possibly do to change it. His own house is protected from the road by a picket fence and an unclipped lilac hedge as well as a new swing gate he designed across the drive after spending the better part of one summer in research by looking at everyone else's gate. By isolating architectural features of the New England landscape in their pure form—like a white gable-peaked arch he designed at the end of a double herbaceous border—Van Valkenburgh forces others to see in them associations with and memories of other places and other times.

For one client who owns houses across the road from each other on Martha's Vineyard, Van

Valkenburgh's additions made it possible for their surrounding spaces to be experienced with fresh eyes. On the oceanfront property, the new cobblestone drive with runoff troughs that impede erosion is a forceful design in itself. But the major innovation, Wrightian in its dynamic form, is an extended stone terrace wall that juts out into the lawn like the prow of a ship. Extending far beyond the weathered Colonial house, it functions as a viewing platform looking out to the panorama of the sea. In the afternoon, it casts a dramatic shadow on the sweep of lawn that circles around it. On the boundary of the property, Van Valkenburgh planted an equally arresting long border of white hydrangeas.

On the land side, the property around a Victorian clapboard house had to be cleared of scruffy growth to carve out a landscape where the lawn again becomes the central focus for the rest of the garden. From the roadside, granite steps framed with indigenous day lilies look like an ordinary entrance, corresponding to porch steps at the end of a bluestone walk. The house is screened from the road by a woodland growth collected from woods including pitch pine, hollies, azalea, and woodbine.

Only after turning the corner of the house is the plan revealed: joined bluestone pavers suddenly become stepping stones embedded in grass. It is a stark design in contrast to the turquoise carpenter's lace of the house. Then simply by using the multiple entrances at the side of the house to determine axes, Van Valkenburgh made a repeated design out of a set of granite steps leading up the slope of the lawn to a terrace and two of the doors. A stone path from the third door crosses the lawn at right angles to the stepping stones; its line is reinforced by a parallel border of Russian sage. And in the corner of the house, a linden viburnum turns brilliant crimson against the green lawn in autumn. Two more sets of granite steps, cut into a fieldstone retaining wall at the far end of the lawn, lead to shaded paths through a dense growth of maples, sweetfern, bayberry, and wild roses.

Though this landscape bears Van Valkenburgh's imprint of hard-edged forms, the shapes and textures of stones as pavers and steps and a typical New England wall crafted by a New

Hampshire stone mason, it reflects the 19th-century aesthetic where even the most simple house was set apart from the village by its own circle of green that merged at its outer edges with the open landscape of the surrounding countryside.

In contrast to these severely architectural designs and because of his extensive work with the photographs of Gertrude Jekyll, Van Valkenburgh is a strong proponent of planted borders. What interests him is the design of borders that direct as well as please the eye. Fascinated with the seasonality of Jekyll's floral selections and the progression of plantings along her garden paths, he reproduced these theories in a plan for a hypothetical corporate garden, a 300-foot herbaceous border, with hundreds of 10-foot-square beds set on the diagonal, separated by grass walkways. Each bed is planted with one kind of flower in shades of pale pink to deep red; the border blooms sequentially, so that color washes over it slowly like a wave from one end to the other, with, for example, a light pink iris, "Vanity," in June, to a deep burgundy dahlia, "Black Narcissus," in July, and on to a silvery pink Japanese anemone, "Robustissima," in August.

For several gardens, he has designed raised parterres with granite curbs. At a house in Minnesota, he planted these with vegetables, herbs, and flowers, while at another garden in Greenwich, for clients seeking plant diversity, he filled them with several varieties of roses and divided one bed from the other with rows of espaliered fruit trees. The beauty of the parterre form is that in winter covered with snow or even barren the open rectangles of stone make a pleasing design on the land.

What is engaging about following Michael Van Valkenburgh's career as a landscape architect and teacher is that his ideas build with his commissions and exposure to new places. For example, a new landscape he designed within a traffic circle for General Mills in Minneapolis could easily have been planted in lawn, "captured lawn," he calls it. But instead he created a prairie encircled by 162 Heritage River birch trees, and each year the grasses are burned off to invigorate future growth. Similarly, although he did not finally win the competition to restore the Tuileries Garden in Paris, his study of Le Nôtre's geometric plantings and his innovative plan—to introduce the topiary cones

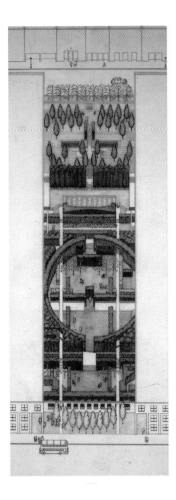

of Sceaux in a series of grids that would have linked the Tuileries to the Place du Carrousel—will continue to affect not only his designs but our own perceptions of that historic space.

Extracting the essence of this French classical garden vocabulary, Van Valkenburgh has created a small interior walled garden for an office building in Paris at 50, avenue Montaigne. Although placed in a contemporary setting, the elements, new and spare—rows of pyramidal hornbeams and espaliered lindens in alternation with long basins of water—evoke the spirit of a young 17th-century garden. What gives it away as a Van Valkenburgh landscape are the stainless steel water columns that terminate the basins as well as the steel runway and viewing platform, and benches designed by Judy McKie in the form of jaguar cats. Where Van Valkenburgh differs from the landscape architect Dan Kiley, who has also acknowledged the influence of Le Nôtre, is in disrupting the geometric order and linear symmetry. Because of some irregular spacing that is his trademark, a crossview of the garden makes the symmetrical arrangement dissolve into a simple bosque of trees. But still, the minimal form of this garden conveys the richness of centuries of French culture.

Van Valkenburgh achieved a similar effect with a birch bosque he designed for a property in Redding, Connecticut, where he planted 60 white spire birch trees in four rows on a slight incline at the edge of some woods. Like the linear Black Granite Garden and the courtyard of 50, avenue Montaigne, the experience of walking among the trees gives the sense of order dissolving only to become ordered again. The only other experience in art that compares with this is watching a corps de ballet dance Balanchine's choreography—just as the dancers give visual satisfaction by lining up, they break ranks into new groups in a constant pattern of resolution and dissolution.

All of this leads to the commission that may be the summit of his career to date, the new Master Plan for the Harvard Yard Landscape. As a sacred space in American history, it compares in importance to the Tuileries in Paris. Van Valkenburgh admits that to alter either of these spaces is like being asked to repaint the Mona Lisa. Still, Harvard is home to Michael Van Valkenburgh, and he speaks of the Yard—a word that has all the connotations of a workaday enclosure attached to purposeful buildings—as an aesthetic unto itself representing Yankee parsimony and elegant frugality.

The challenge for him is how to intervene without making the landscape look significantly revised.

Essentially, the landscape is composed of a ground plane of grass crossed with paths under a high canopy of deciduous trees, a combination, according to Van Valkenburgh, that provides a unique sense of place, a New England commons. The firm's sketches for the project demonstrate that Van Valkenburgh's extensive knowledge of tree planting will be as important to our century as Le Nôtre's was for his. Drawings of the Old Yard show how the central axis will be reinforced with tulip poplar trees and how the general replanting will look with rows of unevenly spaced trees. In the part of the yard called Tercentenary Theater, he plans to develop a central halo of light in the deciduous canopy by planting honey locusts in the center with red oaks and red maples at the periphery.

A view of these gardens and landscapes provides an anthology of a sensibility that is intensely original, modernist, and respectful of the past. I met Michael Van Valkenburgh and first saw a garden of his in 1986 at the Urban Center in New York during an exhibition called "Transforming the American Garden: 12 New Landscape Designs." We stood together next to his submission, a model for a visionary corporate garden called Eudoxia: A New Civic Landscape. It was spatial and sculptural, and it used elements of private gardens like hedges and herbaceous borders in colorful hues that related to the city. But what I remember most was the tissue-paper model for the 25-foot-high ice and water wall and what he said about the sounds of water and the fragrance of moisture. The image of the ice wall is lodged in my imagination as if I had seen it. I missed the real ones he constructed in Radcliffe Yard in the winter of 1988, but I have the newspaper photograph of him in front of them—a spare white glistening veneer. In a kind of magical alchemy, Michael Van Valkenburgh can take old elements and transform them into new visions.

IN THE WORKS

PUBLIC AND CORPORATE DESIGNS

John Beardsley

These are perplexing times for landscape architects, as they are for anyone engaged in contemporary cultural discourse. The rhetoric of modernism is in retreat, challenged on the one hand by a renascent if sometimes too casual historicism, on the other by a thorough-going critique of the largely European and American male culture from which modernism arose. Regardless of how we feel about the changes, there is no question that this critique is an expression of dramatic demographic and social shifts that have brought different and sometimes oppositional voices into the conversation about recent culture. Old hierarchies are yielding to a new pluralism, one that has us speaking, often haltingly, across the frontiers of race, class, ethnicity, and gender.

Especially for the landscape architect working in the public space, these broad cultural changes can't be ignored. But landscape architecture faces other challenges as well, ones more particular to the discipline. As the design profession most obviously linked to the physical environment, it has had to come to grips with a series of profound changes in the way the landscape itself is perceived. Where we might once have been forgiven for seeing it as boundless and bountiful, the willing object of our ambitions and desires, we now must see it as something more fragile and imperiled. More importantly, we have come to recognize it as a complex system of which we are also a part, a system in which our actions have the most serious ecological consequences. For the contemporary landscape architect, reckoning with these changes means inventing a practice that is both scientifically sound and expressive of a land ethic as articulated by recent ecological theorists. It also means learning to love the landscape as we actually inhabit it—debased as it often is—rather than as we know it from fantasy or from myth.

In reinventing their practice, landscape architects have been inspired by the history of their own discipline. One need only look to Frederick Law Olmsted's work in Manhattan's Central Park or the Boston Fens to see dramatic instances of landscape architecture dealing with despoiled spaces. But to some degree, contemporary designers have been prodded as much by the example of recent artists, notably environmental sculptors such as Robert Smithson. It was he, I think, who most provocatively articulated for all of us a post-modern view of the landscape, one in which our patterns of consumption and waste were all too apparent and one in which entropy—a measure of the gradual, steady loss of order in a system—became the prevailing metaphor. Yet the debased landscape was not something that Smithson viewed with despair. Neither was it to be ignored or dismissed. It was rather to be embraced as a positive challenge: "A bleached and fractured world surrounds the artist," Smithson wrote in an essay called "A Sedimentation of the Mind: Earth Projects" in 1968. "To organize this mess of corrosion…is an esthetic process that has scarcely been touched."[1] In addition to challenging some of the more pastoral conventions of landscape, Smithson and his contemporaries bequeathed a richly sculptural language to landscape architecture, one with which the practice is only now beginning to come to terms.

But what, the impatient reader might well be asking now, does all this have to do with Michael Van Valkenburgh, the subject of this text? A lot, I think. As both a teacher and a working designer, Van Valkenburgh inhabits two worlds: one of academic theory and one of actual practice. In the former, he is exposed to the ideas currently reshaping the discipline; in the latter, he faces the test of reconciling those ideas to the real world. To look at Van Valkenburgh's work—especially his designs for corporate clients or for public space—is to see a landscape architect coming to grips with a number of particularly contemporary challenges. It is to be witness to an effort to marry an essentially placeless modernist language with more recent contextual concerns, whether defined in terms of regionalism or local ecology. It is to observe landscape architecture coming to terms with the common, often debased, contemporary landscape. It is also to see the beginnings of a more sculptural approach to space, in which, in the spirit of some recent environ-

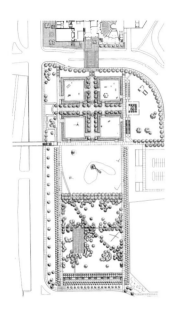

mental art, earth is shaped as much for symbolic as for formal design purposes. All this emerges most clearly in Van Valkenburgh's largest completed public project to date, Mill Race Park in Columbus, Indiana. But these many layers can be traced in other of his projects as well, as they can in the work of a number of his equally interesting contemporaries in the field. Indeed, I think we can take Van Valkenburgh's work as representative in some ways of a discipline in the midst of a significant transformation—from a relatively formalist to a more theoretical and contextual basis; from a predominantly functional and horticultural approach to one that embraces a full range of ecological and symbolic concerns as well.

Van Valkenburgh's roots in a modernist, geometric language are apparent in one of his earliest designs for a civic space. Called Eudoxia, the design was published in *Transforming the American Garden: 12 New Landscape Designs* in 1986. A proposed urban garden for a hypothetical corporate headquarters, Eudoxia was described by its designer as being "in the spirit of early 20th century modernists: abstracted geometric forms and spaces are linked by a broken axis and are balanced by proportion rather than symmetry."[2] Its sources were in modern art, Van Valkenburgh noted, especially in cubism and in the paintings of Laszlo Moholy-Nagy—though a debt to Piet Mondrian and the artists of De Stijl is also apparent in the plan. Van Valkenburgh's preference for classic geometry suggests an affinity as well for the work of Dan Kiley, an affinity borne out, as we shall see, in his Columbus projects.

A number of Van Valkenburgh's recent designs continue to emphasize strong geometric plans. His extension to the Minneapolis Sculpture Garden at the Walker Art Center, completed in 1992, was intended both as a complement and as a counterpoint to the severe, room-like spaces designed for the original garden by Edward Larrabee Barnes and landscape architect Peter Rothschild. Van Valkenburgh continued Barnes's geometry, but began to dissolve it. Most obviously, existing straight rows of trees give way to random plantings. A curved path arcs through space and terminates at one edge; it is balanced asymmetrically by a rectilinear wall at the other side. Van Valkenburgh again used interrupted geometries in an interior courtyard for a corporate build-

ing at 50, avenue Montaigne in Paris, completed in 1993. The basic composition consists of parallel rows of paths, pools, and horizontally plaited linden and European hornbeam trees, with vertical accents provided by stainless steel water columns. This establishes a strong pattern from above
and complex visual layers at eye level, with overlapping rows of trees and columns. The predominantly parallel patterns are broken by a cross axis that enters from the building lobby and leads to
an elevated seating terrace.

Counterpoised to these emphatically geometric works, Van Valkenburgh has executed projects with more obvious ecological and sculptural aspects. For the entrance to the General Mills
Corporate Headquarters in Minneapolis in 1991, he planted a richly-textured landscape of river
birch trees and mixed species of the short-grass prairie. This island of indigenous species goes
unmowed—it is allowed to grow and is burned off once a year. In an otherwise heavily manicured
corporate landscape that is characterized by closely-cropped lawns, Van Valkenburgh's gesture
here can fairly be described as subversive. This landscape reads like a remnant of the original local
ecosystem, or as an emblem of its possible rebirth. In the absence of larger efforts to restore
extensive tracts of the prairie, this space is likely to maintain a decidedly quixotic and somewhat
ironic tone.

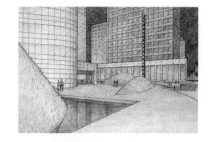

Meanwhile, Van Valkenburgh has begun to explore the sculptural possibilities of landscape as
well. We will see the impact of this sculptural thinking on Mill Race Park, but it can also be detect-
ed in a series of unbuilt projects. One of the most interesting of these has developed over the
past year in collaboration with the sculptor Martin Puryear; it is a proposal for a courtyard at the
New School for Social Research in New York. The proposal is dominated by a raised oval on an
earthen mound, wrapped with a curving ramp. Both these elements have been designed to be
functional—the oval as a stage for small concerts and academic ceremonies; the ramp to provide
access for the handicapped. But the mound is meant to register as much as a sculptural form; this
effect is meant to be enhanced by a group of proposed furnishings in stone and wire to be made
by Puryear. An even more sculptural use of earthen forms can be found in Van Valkenburgh's pro-

posal for the HO-AM Art Museum and Sculpture Garden in Seoul, Korea, also dating from 1993. His original scheme for the site called for a series of whale-like forms set in pools of water, in a landscape of textured grasses and willow trees. Van Valkenburgh's proposal is at once radical and traditional; it was inspired both by the example of recent sculpture and by a composition of round islands in a square pool of water that he saw in a Seoul park.

This attention to historical context is another element of the complex layering that characterizes some of the most compelling designs in contemporary landscape architecture. One of Van Valkenburgh's most thorough investigations of site history came in his proposal for the renovation and extension of the Jardin des Tuileries in Paris. Van Valkenburgh was a participant in an invited competition that resulted in part from the closing of a street that formerly divided the Tuileries from the western courtyard of the Louvre. This gave new impetus to the effort to resolve the ambiguity between the two spaces, which are on different axes. The main thrust of Van Valkenburgh's proposal was to unify the two spaces through an expanded grid of 12-foot-tall evergreen topiary arranged in quincunx pattern on both sides of the former street. To further tie them together, he proposed adding four new circular water basins, two on each side. These would be smaller versions of the existing ones, which were part of André Le Nôtre's original scheme.

Elsewhere in the gardens, Van Valkenburgh proposed other changes. Along the rue de Rivoli, he suggested creating a long, narrow canal garden, meant to evoke the spirit of Le Nôtre's basins at Vaux-le-Vicomte. He also developed a plan to reinvigorate the celebrated but declining grand bosque of horse chestnut trees. He suggested diversifying the monoculture and enhancing the seasonal variation in the bosque by the introduction of four new species of trees. Sycamore maples, paulownia, silver lindens, and sophora (scholar trees), with their various flowering times and foliage characters, would be added in double rows, one species each inside the four opposing pairs of existing "rooms" of horse chestnuts. Overall, Van Valkenburgh's intent for the Tuileries was to remain true to the geometric language of Le Nôtre's original plan, while enhancing both the connection to the courtyard at the Louvre and opportunities for public use.

For the sake of the lucidity of my own argument, I have been presenting sequentially the various strands of Van Valkenburgh's work—formal, ecological, sculptural, and historical—as if they were somehow autonomous. But they typically are not—especially not in his more ambitious recent projects. By way of example, I want to turn now to Van Valkenburgh's largest completed project, Mill Race Park in Columbus, Indiana, to see how the various strands are woven together. The beginnings of this park go back some thirty years, when a group of civic-minded residents started the transformation of 65 acres of derelict flood plain at the western edge of town into a public landscape. The site lies in brushy bottomlands where the Flatrock and Driftwood join to form the East Fork of the White River. Once known as Death Valley, it was originally a place of ramshackle housing scattered around 26 acres of gravel pits and a tannery that belched dead-animal fumes into the air. When the tannery closed in the early 1960s, a group called the River Rats coalesced to begin the creation of the city's first park.

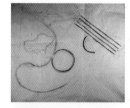

In observance of the quincentennial of the voyage of Christopher Columbus, for whom the town is named, Van Valkenburgh was invited to complete the park, in association with architect Stanley Saitowitz of San Francisco. In the process, the park was enlarged to 85 acres, with the addition of degraded industrial land that was cleansed of toxic residue. Commissioned by the Columbus Parks and Recreation Department, Mill Race Park was constructed primarily by Job Corps trainees, with funds from private citizens and local industry. Design fees were paid by the Cummins Engine Foundation, a local philanthropy that largely has been responsible for making Columbus something of a museum of mid-to-late-twentieth-century architecture and landscape design.

Van Valkenburgh's scheme for the park effectively demonstrates the way in which close attention to local social, historical, and ecological circumstances can be combined with a compelling formal language to create a multi-layered design. This contextualized approach is revealed first of all in Van Valkenburgh's attitude to existing elements of the site. Instead of obliterating the past, he made use of it. Several four-foot-high concrete walls that originally sheltered the tannery from flood waters now screen a parking area from the rest of the park. The two gravel pits have likewise become important landscape features: one has been retained as an irregularly-shaped pond, while the other has been enlarged to become the central visual element in the park, Round Lake.

Van Valkenburgh also made use of "found objects" present at the site, notably several bridges collected by the city engineer. A covered bridge that was long ago moved to the park now crosses the cut between the two lakes. A metal truss bridge spans a low spot near the river, while another stands like a sculpture on high ground. Van Valkenburgh enhanced access to the natural features of the site as well: thick brush was cleared from the riverbank and the tree canopy was raised throughout the park to open eye-level vistas to water. An existing road was moved closer to the river and a pedestrian path was laid out along the water's edge.

Contextualization is also evident in the language of Van Valkenburgh's design. Most notably, he created a transition between the geometry of the town and the irregular contours of the river bank. His plan is most geometric on the city side, where parking lots and three parallel rows of trees are laid out in a grid and traversed by paths at right angles to each other. The geometry not only plays off the grid of town, but also an existing double row of lindens that bracket a playing field in the park. (The lindens were reportedly planted at the suggestion of Dan Kiley during one of his many visits to Columbus to work on the Miller Garden and the North Christian Church.) The simple geometry is reiterated in the perfect regularity of Round Lake, and in the single row of cherry trees around it. But it begins to dissolve almost at once: the rows of trees in the parking area are irregularly spaced; they also turn out to be a random assortment of indigenous species, including hackberry and Kentucky coffee trees. And the geometry is entirely gone from the design by the time it reaches the river, where the perimeter path follows a winding course under existing groves of maple, cottonwood, and sycamore trees.

The 450-foot-diameter Round Lake is the pivot on which the entire design turns. Its scale and formal authority are such that it may dwarf the ring of cherries even in their maturity, but Van Valkenburgh opted against a double row to retain the openness of the view to the river. Around the lake, as Van Valkenburgh says, "the park is ordered through circulation and a program of activities" such as ball courts and playing fields, an amphitheater, a playground, a boat landing, and a wetlands interpretation area. "It is also marked throughout by follies," he adds, referring to a family of architectural structures designed by Saitowitz that includes a performance stage, an 80-foot tower, picnic shelters, rest rooms, two fishing piers, a boat house, and an arbor, all of which are related to each other in form and material. All are handsomely and practically constructed from red steel tubing, concrete, glass block, and corrugated metal, and appropriately share a language of simple geometry with Van Valkenburgh's landscape design. Saitowitz describes some of them as "use specific," such as the rest rooms and the stage, and some as "site specific," such as the tower that marks the terminus of the city's 5th Street axis at the river. The tower also makes the entrance of the park visible from the town, from which it is separated by a busy street and railroad tracks.

Van Valkenburgh's use of the word "folly" to refer to these structures is somewhat confusing. Historically, the term implies a kind of extravagance and uselessness; it is also associated with aristocratic patrons. "I was actually reacting against the traditional idea of a folly," Saitowitz says, "reinterpreting it in terms of a contemporary park for public use, not for the elite. It's quite a rough context. I wanted to make pieces that have no history," he continued, to change traditional forms while retaining "public legibility." Despite their unusual materials and wavy roofs, his restrooms and picnic shelters are obviously what they are. So too is the arbor, despite the fact that it is formed not from wooden trellis but from hoops of red steel. And rather than being covered in plants, it is roofed in perforated metal, creating a dappled light within.

For the most part, Van Valkenburgh and Saitowitz worked separately on their parts of the park design. But they did collaborate on a massive, crescent-shaped berm that doubles on one side as a terraced amphitheater for the performance stage. This berm is one of three sculpted earthworks in the landscape: another contains a basketball court, and a third rises above the pond and provides views over park. "The mounds are conceived as prospects," Van Valkenburgh explains, noting that there are few elevated spots in the city or surrounding countryside. "But they also make reference to the tradition of mound-making in this landscape," alluding to the prehis-toric creations of Native American cultures throughout the Ohio Valley. As such, Van Valkenburgh wanted them to have an "enigmatic" quality. But, here, the layering that otherwise makes the park so interesting becomes problematic. The sculptural and symbolic power of the largest of these mounds is diminished by the fact that it doubles as a functional element. Even from the opposite side, the top of the stage peeks over the hill, undercutting the otherwise won-derful sense of enigma.

In the spirit of Robert Smithson, Van Valkenburgh relished the particular challenge of this abused and flood-prone site. The mounds, for example, were conceived to have an informal rela-tionship to each other, which will become apparent during flooding when they, the covered bridge, and the treetops will be all that is visible of the park. At that point, Van Valkenburgh expects the mounds to look like accidental elements of the scene, "like flotsam." The certainty of flooding gave rise to other design decisions: the playground is elevated on an earthen platform, so it will stay dry during high water, and the walls of the restrooms are raised off the ground to allow the waters to wash through. The experience of working on Mill Race Park has led Van Valkenburgh to see great promise in recasting other marginal lands as public open space. "It's the future," he insists. "Every community has a derelict piece of land, often along a river, that they don't think of as being usable." Like Smithson, Van Valkenburgh sees the potential for recycling these landscapes to both artistic and public ends.

Mill Race Park is just one part of Van Valkenburgh's work for Columbus. He has also devel-oped a master plan for the principal entry to the city from the west, along the corridor that leads from Interstate 65 over the White River into downtown. This entry will lead to other parts of the city landscaped by Van Valkenburgh, including the grounds of the county courthouse and the 5th Street corridor, which in turn gives access to Mill Race Park. The variety and extent of Van Valkenburgh's efforts in Columbus have strengthened his commitment to working in the public realm. While he laments the relative lack of funding for such projects in recent years as cities everywhere cope with shrinking tax bases and declining federal revenues, he celebrates the "civic compo-nent" of the public space: "you're making something everybody in the community gets to use."

At the same time, Van Valkenburgh has had to marry this understanding of the social dimen-sions of the public space both to a personal design language and to a complex and sensitive read-ing of the various characteristics of a given site, whether physical or cultural. Depending on which party in this union carries the most weight, Van Valkenburgh's work to date has ranged in expres-sion from the emphatically geometric to the candidly ecological, from the graphic to the sculptural. It is no doubt an expression of his maturation that so many of these dimensions of design come together at Mill Race Park. Like a number of his contemporaries, Van Valkenburgh is taking a rela-tively placeless modernist language and reconciling it to context, exploring not just the formal and functional elements of landscape but the social, historical, and symbolic ones as well. He is likewise coming to terms with the despoiled, even entropic common landscape. Michael Van Valkenburgh, somewhat like the profession itself, seems to be on the way to finding a complex and authorita-tive contemporary voice.

[1] Robert Smithson, "A Sedimentation of the Mind: Earth Projects," in Nancy Holt, ed., *The Writings of Robert Smithson* (New York: New York University Press, 1979): 82.

[2] Michael R. Van Valkenburgh, "Eudoxia: A New Civic Landscape," in *Transforming the American Garden: 12 New Landscape Designs* (Cambridge, MA: Harvard University Graduate School of Design, 1986): 20.

All other quotations are taken from recent conversations.

PROJECTS

MILL RACE PARK

Columbus, Indiana 1989–1993

Mill Race Park occupies 85 acres at the western edge of downtown Columbus within the flood plain of the East Fork of the White River. Initially, the park was a 66 acre wooded area that was developed as open space over the last 25 years by community volunteers. An additional 19 acres of adjacent land, added in 1990, was used previously for industrial purposes. Michael Van Valkenburgh Associates provided master planning and complete design services for the park. The park buildings were programmed by the firm and sited in collaboration with architect Stanley Saitowitz, who designed the park architecture.

The design strives to reinvigorate the American park as the centerpiece of public life and as a symbol of the spirit of Columbus. From its inception

the design of Mill Race Park developed within an open and inclusive framework that involved public leaders, interested citizens, and local government. The project elements included a performance amphitheater to accommodate up to 5,000; a round lake and a boat house; three picnic shelters; a large playground; a basketball court; a fishing pier; horseshoe pits; two rest rooms; parking lots for 600 cars; connection of the existing People Trail with a new half-mile River Walk; park lighting; and a wetlands interpretive area.

The Round Lake provides a spiritual center for the park and expresses the built form of the city through the pure geometry of the circle juxtaposed with the sinuous forms of the surrounding rivers. A widely spaced row of flowering cherry trees marks the perimeter of the lake.

The design stresses the experiential quality of the park spaces and the river edge. A new river walk connects with an existing network of trails that links the downtown with outlying neighborhoods. The park loop road was relocated closer to the river to allow motorists to look out over the water. Editing the existing vegetation revealed the underlying ecology of the flood plain and established a connection between the park and its context. The industrial history of Columbus and its relationship to the river are engaged in the design by revealing on site fragments of industrial building foundations and the inclusion of new and visible infrastructure.

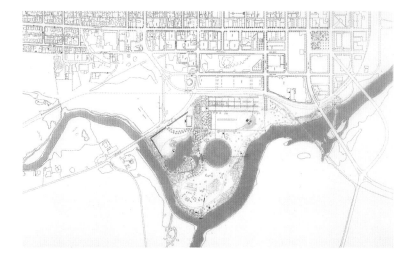

Chautauqua Arts Festival

opposite, Round Lake

opposite, amphitheater

sluice

lawn and tree rows

*boat house, dam, and
boat landings*

*opposite,
basketball court*

Oakville, Ontario, Canada 1993

The site for this invited competition is a 45-acre tract of public open space in a rapidly growing suburban city west of Toronto. The competition, sponsored by the Town of Oakville, called on entrants to design the three parcels of land that make up the site. The competition guidelines also required on-site storm water management for the entire development.

The design treats the site as three distinct urban landscapes—a natural park, a public garden, and a civic square. These three elements are linked by a linear forest along the north edge. The 30-meter-wide forest contains an informal planting of native, high-branched deciduous and evergreen trees.

The park includes wetlands, low hummocks, lakes, groves, a ravine, and a large prospect hill. The hill rises 12 meters above the street and provides a large lawn that can serve as a concert space. The wetlands and lakes are part of a storm water purification and retention system that is intended to visibly express the infrastructure of the park. A circular, two-stage settling pool utilizes aquatic plants to remove nutrients and sediments from incoming storm water that is then transferred via an open sluiceway to the wetlands system. The changing water level creates moisture gradients needed to yield a diverse regime of vegetation and wildlife. Michael Van Valkenburgh Associates collaborated with Landplan of Toronto.

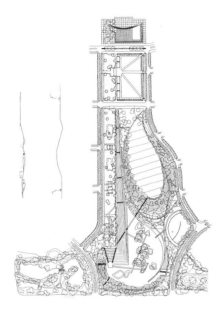

opposite, constructed
wetlands and linear
forest, rendering

public lawn, rendering

study model of earth
forms and wetlands

Michael Van Valkenburgh and Barbara Stauffacher Solomon were hired as a team to design the Regis Gardens for the Cowles Conservatory in the Minneapolis Sculpture Garden, a project of the Walker Art Center and the Minneapolis Parks and Recreation Board. The garden's first exterior phase—designed by Peter Rothschild and Edward Larrabee Barnes—opened in 1988.

The only "given" inside the tripartite conservatory, also designed by the office of Edward Larrabee Barnes, was Frank Gehry's 22-foot-high *Standing Glass Fish* (1986), placed by Van Valkenburgh and Solomon to emerge from a small lily pond in the conservatory's central house. With the configuration of the conservatory's elongated north and south wings and square central house as parameters, the designers were free to create three interior gardens. They developed a sequence of green arches—topiaries of ficus vines with flower beds beneath—for the north house, a palm and orange tree central court surrounding Gehry's fish, and a series of stainless steel wire trellises for flowering vines in the south house.

While that work was being completed, Van Valkenburgh was engaged to design a 4.5-acre addition to the 7.5-acre sculpture garden, in collaboration with the Art Center's director Martin Friedman. "The aspect of the environment that was most critical in Minneapolis was, of course, the presence of the original 1988 garden," Van Valkenburgh explains. "The challenges presented by the first garden were its formality and symmetry and the roomlike character of its spaces, which are surrounded by twelve-foot-high green hedges." In such defined gallerylike spaces, works interact and installations are created. It was agreed that, by contrast, the expansion should have an exploded grove of trees to establish more informal boundaries, allowing the sculptures a certain autonomy.

A second challenge in designing the garden's expansion was that the site is bounded on two sides by heavily trafficked highways. Thus, a sound wall was inserted into the evergreen spruce hedgerow that surrounds the expansion area and the central greensward containing the *Spoonbridge and Cherry* fountain and pond by Claes Oldenburg and Coosje van Bruggen. The double row of spruce trees that once formed a backdrop for the *Spoonbridge* was moved to the perimeter of the site and the fountain has become a crossroads in the expanded garden. Behind it is a loosely planted grove of deciduous native Minnesota trees that permits a view through the entire length of the garden. A fifteen-foot-high vine-covered stainless steel arbor serves as a terminus to the northern end of the site.

Mildred Friedman (**MF**)

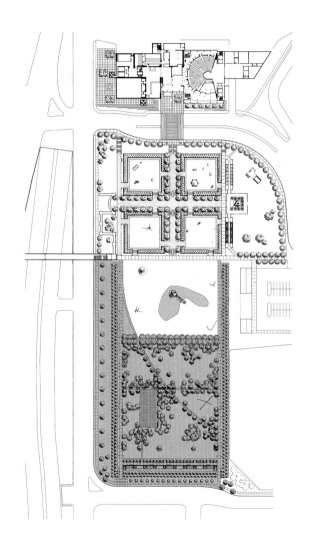

*previous page, views
from the arbor,
September 1993*

garden in 1992

garden in 2012

curved entry walk

performance festival

North House, topiary arches

South House, vine scrims

Michael Van Valkenburgh Associates and Kyu Sung Woo Associates, project architects, developed a master plan for the entire eighty-five acre site. A museum of Korean antiquities exists on the site and a museum of contemporary art is also proposed. HO-AM is a landscape reclamation project—little of the natural landscape remains in a site that has been insensitively reworked to create a parking area.

The client requested a landscape suitable for an international collection of contemporary sculpture not yet in place. Van Valkenburgh proceeded "by amassing a fictional sculpture collection in our office—di Suveros, Puryears, Moores, Sheas, Calders—and then we set about making a set of landscape conditions to accommodate gallery-scale pieces as well as larger site-specific works."

The climate in Korea is difficult: very icy in winter and the summers are monsoon hot. When it rains the site will become a water garden as, in typical Korean fashion, water will be collected in open swales along the pathways. Using a series of pools and water gardens beside a restored stream, a reconfigured lake edge, and a new wetlands zone, Van Valkenburgh has designed a garden whose topography and water will create a rich variety of spaces for sculpture.

MF

site model

constructed wetlands and water canal

opposite, sculpture terraces

General Mills Headquarters is located in a hilly suburban landscape with almost no trees and many acres of mowed industrial grass. Michael Van Valkenburgh Associates was commissioned to redesign the area at the main entrance to provide an appropriate setting for a ten-foot-high bronze work by sculptor Mel Kendrick and to develop a more inviting entrance to the headquarters.

In this area Van Valkenburgh chose to plant a field of short native grasses and wildflowers beneath a dense perimeter grove of 162 Heritage River birch trees. Three species of grasses were used: prairie dropseed, little bluestem, and Pennsylvania sedge. Because he wanted huge drifts of color only three species of wildflowers were chosen: lupins, to bloom in June, butterfly weed for July, and rough blazing star for late summer. The grass field is burned at the end of winter and allowed to grow anew each year.

A flame-finished, gray granite walk establishes the main entry for visitors to the central office complex. A gravel path perpendicular to the granite walk allows access to Kendrick's sculpture and to other nearby sculpture display areas.

MF

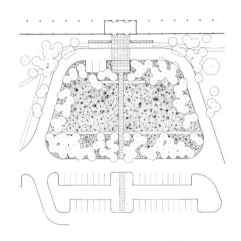

birch trees

prairie burn

opposite, garden in winter

opposite, shortgrass prairie with rough blazing star

garden from roof of building with Kendrick's sculpture

MASTER PLAN FOR THE HARVARD YARD LANDSCAPE

Cambridge, Massachusetts 1993

Harvard Yard is the spiritual center of the Harvard University campus. More than three centuries of architecture and built landscape form an inseparable composition in which architecture delimits the spaces and landscape defines the ground surfaces, characterizes internal enclosures, and marks the sky above. The physical structure of the Yard landscape has recently deteriorated. American elms that once gracefully defined the overhead tree canopy have succumbed to Dutch elm disease. Michael Van Valkenburgh Associates was asked to produce a master plan that would direct the evolution of Harvard Yard over the next decade. The plan was approved in August 1993 and Phase One was implemented in spring 1994.

Harvard Yard, one of the oldest, continually used built landscapes in the United States, stands as an icon of American history. The master plan provides a framework for understanding this built landscape and directing its physical change through a synthetic critique of the relationships of space, materials, and culture while respecting the frugal elegance of its materiality that has guided its evolution over time.

Three primary areas of investigation include the replanting of the Yard's tree canopy; a revision of circulation systems, based on current demands and anticipated building use changes; and revising many inappropriate late recent projects.

Tercentenary Theater at commencement

opposite, view of Harvard Yard near 1857 Gate

view of Harvard Yard from Johnston Gate

Following a National Endowment for the Arts grant to Michael Van Valkenburgh to study climatic effects on ice formation, the Harvard/Radcliffe Office for the Arts commissioned a temporary installation of ice walls in Radcliffe Yard. The design consisted of three arcing walls, each measuring fifty feet long and seven feet high and constructed of a fine galvanized metal mesh with a thin irrigation pipe running along the top. Water emitted from the irrigation system froze and created walls of ice.

KRAKOW ICE GARDEN

Martha's Vineyard, Massachusetts 1990

The design for the garden of this private residence celebrates the changing seasons as experienced on the coast of Massachusetts through the semi-transparent and translucent qualities of plants and ice. Beginning in spring, purple clematis bloom on the 38-foot-diameter circle of steel mesh, followed by blue morning glory in summer, and the red of Boston ivy in autumn. In the winter, a drip irrigation system causes walls of ice to form on the scrim. Within the circle are raised French planting beds.

Paris 1991

This project is an effort to refurbish Paris's earliest public park and to create a garden for eighteen Aristide Maillol sculptures. The Tuileries Garden, reconfigured in 1666 by André Le Nôtre, is just north of the newly renovated Louvre. In part due to recent changes there, and in part because of inherent problems of age and evolving needs, an international invited competition was staged to change the Tuileries from a royal court to a civic landscape and to create a new connection between the Louvre and the Tuileries.

Since the destruction of the Tuileries Palace in 1871, the area between the Louvre's Carrousel Gardens and the Tuileries has been unresolved. Therefore, that space was a major focus of Van Valkenburgh's proposal. For it he suggested a field of evergreen topiary cones arranged in a quincunx plan to provide spaces for the Maillol sculptures. Van Valkenburgh's scheme also proposed the addition of a demonstration urban fish farm in the form of a long basin along the rue de Rivoli. The spiritual center of the plan is Le Nôtre's series of "Rooms of Light" that chronicle the changing seasons and times of day, located within the restored grand bosque of horse chestnut trees.

The overall goal of the scheme was to acknowledge and preserve the historical importance of the garden while responding to the current needs of the city's residents and visitors.

MF

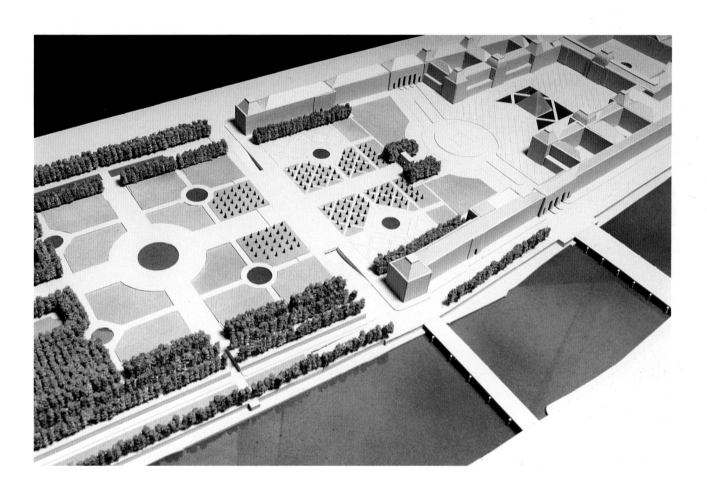

*restored horse chestnut
bosque, photo collage*

*public lawn, new water
basins, and quincunx
topiary, model*

site model

topiary with Maillol sculpture, photo collage

opposite, experimental fish farm along the rue de Rivoli, photo collage

The site is an enclosed courtyard constructed at grade but on the rooftop of a parking garage in an office complex in central Paris. The courtyard garden at the center of the building is a spare composition of stainless steel water columns and long water basins that alternate with rows of columnar hornbeam trees and espaliered linden trees. Though modern in its seriality, the garden borrows elements from French formal gardens. The design principles of layering, parallel composition, and axial ordering were serially applied to the landscape materials of stone, metal, water, and plants to create a garden that draws the viewer into and through its spaces.

In order to make a landscape on a rooftop, extensive site adaptations were required including the creation of low-weight soil mixtures, subsurface drainage, and a complex irrigation system. While this garden was designed to be of visual interest when viewed from the offices above, it is primarily through experience and movement in the courtyard that the landscape is revealed. The building's interior circulation corridor, which is walled in glass, serves as a transparent threshold to the garden space.

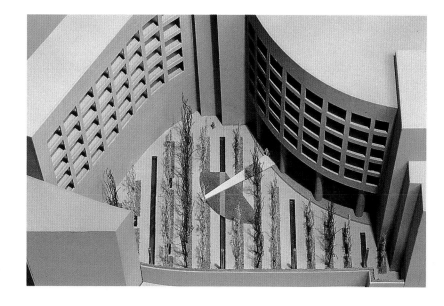

model

*allées of espaliered
lindens and columnar
hornbeam trees*

*opposite, plant rows
at water basins with
benches by Judy McKie*

raised terrace

opposite, water column

opposite, allée

courtyard entrance

BLACK GRANITE GARDEN

Los Angeles, California 1991

An elegant private garden was created by Van Valkenburgh for art collectors whose primary focus is contemporary British sculpture. Adjacent to a large flower garden, the sculpture garden is only 2,500 square feet overall, and thus its elements are scaled to its relatively small size. The landscape architect maintains that in Los Angeles cypress trees are consistently used as boundary planes—seldom to define space. He wanted to use them to make space and so he generated an expanded grid in which the very narrow cypress trees occur about seven feet apart in one direction and fifteen feet apart in the other. The trees are located at the cross points of the grid in three rows. An aerial hedge, created with ficus trees that have been limbed very high, encloses the west side of the garden. Behind them is a galvanized mesh scrim for jasmine and Boston ivy that runs the length of the garden. Paths of crushed black granite lead to the sculptures and a central terrace is formed of cracked black granite and manganese bricks.

The heart of the garden is a twelve-foot-tall, two-foot-wide water wall cut from the same quarry stone used for the terrace. A slow film of water runs over the washboard-like surface and the water moves in and out of its crenellations. Trees, paving, paths, water, and sculpture together create an exceptionally calm, cool environment suited to the pleasure of quiet contemplation.

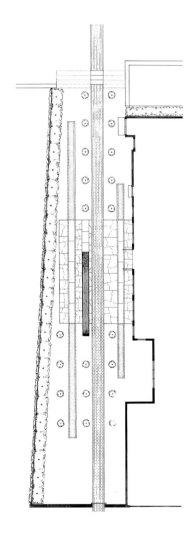

MF

opposite, water channel

principal axis

water planting

COURTYARD

THE NEW SCHOOL FOR SOCIAL RESEARCH

New York, New York 1993–

Michael Van Valkenburgh Associates and the sculptor Martin Puryear were commissioned to redesign the existing courtyard to provide informal seating and gathering spaces, handicapped access, and to introduce more planting and other forms of seasonal notation.

The design constructs an entirely new ground plane for the courtyard. The floor of the connecting foyer space of the 12th Street building is extended into the court and becomes the top level of a large stair into a space that will also function as informal seating. A gently sloping walkway circles around a mound-like landform planted with a grove of small deciduous trees and provides barrier- and railing-free access for wheelchair users. An oval terrace on the mound serves as a dais for lectures, small concerts, and academic ceremonies. A dense perimeter planting of bamboo frames the east side of the courtyard and creates a background for a curved, double-height sitting stair. Construction is expected to begin in the summer of 1995.

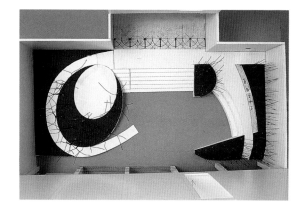

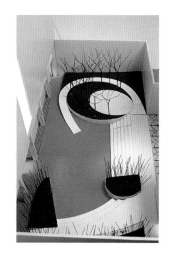

model

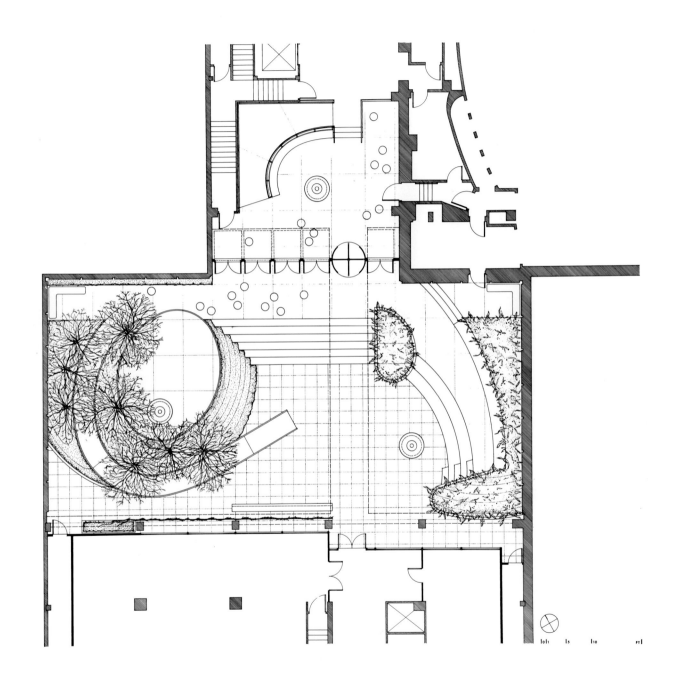

SACKLER SCULPTURE GARDEN

Greenwich, Connecticut 1992

The site is a small enclosed courtyard located adjacent to a late 1940s modernist house. The client requested a small courtyard garden to display two sculptures by Barbara Hepworth. The design for this courtyard creates a supporting ground for the sculpture by reducing architectural details and the planting palette to functional minimums. The composition was simplified to reveal the balance between the permanence of the sculpture and the temporal forces of nature. The spare planting palette created a minimalist aesthetic that reflected the character of the landscape context and engaged the architecture. Small disconnected pieces of lawn were replaced with a continuous ground cover. An existing reflecting pool was redesigned and animated with three low water jets.

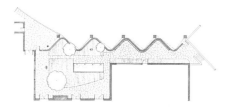

The design for this garden emphasizes the union of plants and formal geometries to reveal relationships of place and time. Straight rows of Black Hills spruce, arborvitae, and a lilac bosque, an arcing band of crocus, a rectangular kitchen garden, and an irregular grove of sugar maple trees all serve to figure the landscape spaces and to objectify the seasonality of the region. Plantings in the raised beds bloom in seasonal succession starting with spring near the house and progressing toward the lake in fall. In winter, the empty raised beds retain the formal aspects of the garden while echoing the region's growing period. Combined, these elements contribute to a cultural understanding of regional garden typologies and the experiential qualities of place. Harrison Fraker was the project architect.

SMALL HOUSE

Martha's Vineyard, Massachusetts 1986

The landscape design for this early 20th-century shore house maintains the simplicity of its original street landscape and includes common seashore plants. To the south side, existing woodland was removed to create a new lawn area that is pressed into the hillside and retained with stepped stone walls. Above the walls, the forest edge was reconstructed with sweet fern, native roses, oaks, and red maples. A south-facing terrace against the house creates a sunny and wind-protected outdoor space that is comfortable from March through November. William Rawn was the project architect.

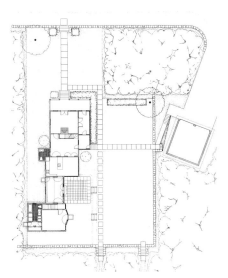

opposite, the void of the lawn affords a place to register shadows and other phenomena

garden wall

front walk

CHESTNUT HILL GARDEN

Brookline, Massachusetts 1986

The design for this residential garden creates a one-quarter acre sunken grove in an urban environment. A brick terrace overlooks the plantings of white and gray birch, common periwinkle, interrupted fern, royal fern, European ginger, mountain laurel, and Canadian hemlock. A flight of wooden stairs constructed over the groundcover leads from the terrace to an irregular glade punctuated by a green granite water column. Two neon light fixtures designed by the landscape architect cast a low level glow over the garden at night.

axonometric rendering

water column

opposite, stairs through birch grove

PUCKER GARDEN

Brookline, Massachusetts 1990

The garden, located at the back of a traditional 1915 brick house, is one-half acre and is situated on a steep slope. The clients requested a new garden to display a collection of small sculptures.

The design of the Pucker Garden is built on the four basic elements of landscape-making: the importance of sequenced spatial structure, the power of earth form, the evocative temporal qualities of plants, and the tactile characteristics of mineral and metal elements. The asymmetrical spatial volumes of the garden are organized along an axis that originates at the street with an entry walk, passes through the house, continues into the lower terrace of the new garden and up the slope with a metal stair. A bowl of space, formed by the excavation of the existing hillside, allows air and light to fill the new garden. The asymmetry of this earthen form establishes a visual tension with the axial walk and metal stair.

A curved walk on the upper level of the garden provides elevated vantage points for viewing the garden, the sculpture, and the house. Approximately two-thirds of the upper perimeter of the garden and the entire northeast edge of the lower lawn next to the house are veiled by seven-foot-tall translucent scrims of galvanized wire mesh. Granite bases for the sculpture are placed on the slope of the bowl, near the curved walk.

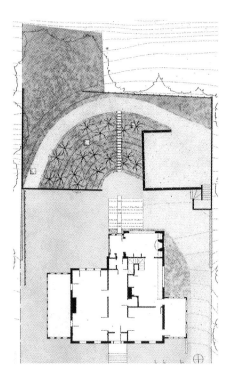

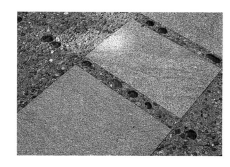

scrim wall

checkerplate stairs

terrace

I am deeply indebted to many, many people without whom the works included in this book would not have been possible; the list of employees who have helped is only a partial acknowledgment. In particular, I want to thank Carol Doyle Van Valkenburgh for listening to and helping to resolve my deliberations about design, which inevitably came home with me from the office. The associates in my office—Laura Solano, Tim Barner, and Matt Urbanski—have been remarkably helpful and have been the frequent providers of formative evolutions of the designs. Special thanks are extended to Todd Rader, who drew many of the perspectives in this book; to Tim Darr, who built many of the models; and especially to Allan Shearer, who helped me write the project statements and served as organizer of the visual material. Leslie Donovan and Alex Barrett also helped in ways that were innumerable and invaluable.

I would like to thank my clients for their support and encouragement and for all that I have learned about the landscape because of their questions and concerns. I also thank Peter G. Rowe, Dean of the Faculty of Design at Harvard University, for his generous and continuing support of this project. The critical contributions of John Beardsley, James Corner, Paula Deitz, Mildred Friedman, Will Miller, and Peter Rowe are enormously appreciated and will be a source of reflection in my future work. Finally, I dedicate this book to Ann M. Elliot, my drawing teacher at Cornell, who taught me to see and who opened my eyes to the magic and mystery of the landscape.

Michael Van Valkenburgh

Principal

Michael Van Valkenburgh

Associates

Timothy Barner

Laura Solano

Matthew Urbanski

Design Staff

Julie Bargmann

William George Batchelor

James P. Cogliano

Sally Elizabeth Coyle

James H. Curtis

Timothy John Darr

Tobias Dayman

Timothy M. Downing

James Nelson Hayter

Ann Hedgepeth

Richard T. Johnson

Joseph MacDonald

Regan McClellan

Eric Mullendore

Tom Oslund

John Peterson

Jeffrey Piskula

Todd Rader

Christopher Reed

Brian K. Rojo

Charlie Rose

Anne Marie Sadowski

Allan Shearer

Carol Souza

Mary Ann Thompson

Carol Doyle Van Valkenburgh

Sam Williamson

Jane Wolff

Staff

Marcia Altman

Joshua Baridge

Alexander Owen Barrett

Jo Robinson Jenkins

Ann Farrington Reis

John Beardsley is a writer and a curator. His books include *Earthworks and Beyond: Contemporary Art in the Landscape* and *Art in Public Places*. He is presently completing the manuscript for a book on environments by visionary artists, to be called *Gardens of Revelation*. He has organized exhibitions on Hispanic Art, Black Folk Art, and Art and the Rain Forests. He is currently associate curator for the exhibition "Landscape as Metaphor," which opens at the Denver Art Museum in May 1994. Beardsley has taught in the landscape architecture programs at the University of Virginia, Harvard University, and the University of Pennsylvania.

James Corner is Assistant Professor of Landscape Architecture at the Graduate School of Fine Arts, University of Pennsylvania, where he teaches design studios and offers seminars in landscape architectural theory and representation. His writings have been published in *Landscape Journal*, *Word and Image*, and *Landscape Architecture*. He is the author of *Taking Measures Across the American Landscape*, with photographs by Alex MacLean and based on the exhibition of the same name, forthcoming from Yale University Press in 1995.

Paula Deitz, co-editor of *The Hudson Review*, writes frequently about landscape architecture for *The New York Times* and other publications.

Mildred Friedman was the design curator at the Walker Art Center from 1970–1991, where she organized numerous exhibitions dealing with architecture and design and edited *Design Quarterly*. She participated in the design of the Minneapolis Sculpture Garden and is currently a design consultant to the Battery Park City Authority, New York.

Will Miller, Chairman of the Irwin Financial Corporation, Columbus, Indiana, was a member of the community committee that oversaw the design process for Mill Race Park—a public project supported in part by the Cummins Engine Foundation. He is a member of the board of directors of Cummins Engine Foundation, among other corporations and not-for-profit groups.

Peter G. Rowe, Raymond Garbe Professor of Architecture and Urban Design and Dean of the Faculty of Design at Harvard University, is the author of *Making a Middle Landscape* (1991), *Design Thinking* (1987), and coauthor of *Principles for Local Environmental Management* (1978). His latest book, *Modernity and Housing* was published by The MIT Press in 1993.

Michael Van Valkenburgh, Professor in Practice of Landscape Architecture and Chairman of the department of Landscape Architecture at the Harvard University Graduate School of Design, is the principal of Michael Van Valkenburgh Associates, a Cambridge-based landscape architecture firm. The firm's designs have received numerous ASLA design awards and, in 1988, Van Valkenburgh was a Design Fellow at the American Academy in Rome. He received the BS in landscape architecture from Cornell University and the MLA from the University of Illinois at Urbana-Champaign.

Adams, Howard. Review of "Transforming the American Garden: 12 New Landscape Designs," *House and Garden* (January 1987): 32-33.

Beardsley, John. "Mill Race Park: Rescuing 'Death Valley'," *Landscape Architecture* (September 1993): 38-43.

———. "Museum Landscapes: More Space for Sculpture," *Landscape Architecture* (January 1992): 62-66.

Campbell, Robert. Review of exhibition "Transforming the American Garden: 12 New Landscape Designs" shown at the Architectural League of New York from February 17–March 14, 1986 and Harvard University Graduate School of Design from April 1–18, 1986, *The Boston Globe*, March 1986.

———. "Winning Plans for Copley Square," *The Boston Globe*, 6 November 1984.

Deitz, Paula. "Landscapes That Recall Rural Simplicity," *The New York Times*, 5 November 1987.

Feinberg, Jean E. "The Museum As Garden," *Landscape Architecture* (April 1989): 68-73.

———. "Transforming the American Garden." An exhibition review. *Landscape Architecture* (July/August 1986): 48-57.

Fleming, Lee. "Long-Term Dividends," *Garden Design* (September/October 1993): 39-49.

Frey, Susan, *et al.* Critical debate about the entries in exhibition and publication "Transforming the American Garden: 12 New Landscape Designs," *Places* 3, no. 3 (1986): 42-59.

Holtz Kay, Jane. "Metal Machine Garden," *Landscape Architecture* (October 1992): 84-88.

Johnson, Jory. "Altered Perceptions," *Garden Design* (Autumn 1984): 56-59.

———. "Arch/Angle," *Garden Design* (Autumn 1983): 42-47.

———. "The Flowering of New England," *House and Garden* (August 1986): 75-77.

———. "P/A Profile: Michael Van Valkenburgh," *Progressive Architecture* (July 1989): 72-77.

Kahn, Eve. "Uncovering the Waterfront," *The Wall Street Journal*, 30 December 1992.

Leviseur, Elsa. "Avant-Garde Ecology," *The Architectural Review* CXCI, no. 1147 (September 1992): 53-58

Littlefield, Susan. "Designer's Choice: 15 North American Landscape Designers," in *Garden Design* (New York: Simon & Schuster, 1984).

Mitani, Toru. "American Landscape Architects," *SD* (Summer 1988): 40-51.

Phillips, Patricia C. Review of exhibition "Transforming the American Garden: 12 New Landscape Designs," *Art Forum* (September 1986): 137.

Sutro, Dirk. "A Garden Sculpted for Art," *Garden Design* (March/April 1991): 109-112.

Yang, Linda. "Built Landscapes at Wave Hill," *The New York Times*, 11 August 1984.

We would like to thank the following photographers:

Ron Bowen, page 46 (right)

Darren Cummins, pages 26, 30

Mark Darley, pages 53, 64, 65

Timothy Darr, page 66

Hervé Abbadie, pages 58 (right), 59, 60, 61, 62, 63

Tom Hysell, pages 39, 41 (left), 42, 43, 47, 49, 69

Charles Mayer, pages 14, 24, 32, 37, 44, 45, 52, 58 (left), 71, 73, 74, 75, 76, 77

Michael Moran, title page and pages 11 (lower), 68

Joe Wrinn, pages 17, 50 (right)

Cover images and additional photography by Michael Van Valkenburgh

EDITOR
Brooke Hodge

DESIGN
Alice Hecht, Hecht Design

DESIGN ASSISTANT
Sarah Smith

PRODUCTION COORDINATION
Susan McNally

RESEARCH ASSISTANT
Allan Shearer

COMPUTER SCANS
Craig Verzone

PRINTER
Friesen Printers
Altona, Manitoba
Canada

The text of this book was set in Adobe Gill Sans and Adobe Garamond using QuarkXPress 3.2.
The cover is printed on Warren Lustro Offset Enamel gloss. The text paper stock is Potlatch Quintessence dull.